To Bryan
With tremendous love and
respect.
    Merry Christmas
        1996
    Love,
    Mother + John

NORTHERING

NORTHERING

NEW AND COLLECTED POEMS

BY HAROLD CORBIN

THE STINEHOUR PRESS

1995

FOREWORD

Most who glance at this small book, let alone read around in it will sense the presence of a friend.

From my earliest reading days, the influence of Robert Frost on whatever intellectual, literary, philosophical and educational pretensions I have has been considerable. With the quickening march of years, that influence has been steadily magnified. During the last decade of his life, in 1957 and in 1961, he honored us by joining our household to become, as he once said of himself, a kind of "poetic radiator" for the boys of Lake Forest Academy in Illinois, a boys' college preparatory boarding school of which I was then headmaster. Those fleeting and glorious weeks were a matchless experience for the Corbin family and friends, to say nothing of the Academy students. For me it was deliriously exhausting; as administrator I spent the days at my duties, the nights listening, for Robert's prime time was after the witching hour. Once he was wound up, sleep was of no interest to him. For me it was unthinkable.

From these magical sessions, as well as from my early reading, and later teaching of his work, his cadences and concepts struck deep. One mutual passion was the structure and function of metaphor, that imperative two-ness which is the true nature of creative tension, and the lifeblood of art and poems—indeed, of the whole symbolic system called language, once defined as the chief instrument of man's humanity. I wanted to say these things at the outset of this small amateurish volume born in the awareness of a certain winged chariot and the nagging urge to leave something lying around the house for friends and weekend guests—before I sleep. It has arrived by the vanity route, not by merit, or speculation of gain; and if any judgment at all should be pronounced upon parts of it, especially that they be suspiciously imitative, I now so proclaim it with pride. This may be one of the virtues of vanity, of which Robert had enough to appreciate the implicit flattery of even my imitation.

In any case this book, together with my lovely anvils, my stoneware, tool and iron collections, and a few birds in wood I leave for the contemplation of my beloved wife and family, my friends and former students, especially Tom. Where I am headed I suspect that none of these impedimenta, with the possible exception of the anvils, is admissible.

H. C.

ACKNOWLEDGMENTS

For instruction, example, love and labor on behalf of these poems, my gratitude, deep and humble, is due

My wife Florie, a co-sufferer, midwife and fearlessly effective watchdog over my verbalizing, rhymed or otherwise

The persisting presence of Robert Frost and all he meant to us

David McCord, who gave priceless hours of counsel, for which my gratitude is exceeded only by the depth of our friendship

Joseph Blumenthal, for his warm friendship, wisdom, and professional guidance in my first venture into the world of printing, an art to which I have every intention of devoting my career next time around

Tom Harris, for his patient fellowship and knowledgeable criticism

And, finally, to generations of my students and surrogate sons who, more than they ever suspected, were the real teachers and fathers in my life.

[7]

For

TOM HARRIS

former student,
fellow poet &
cherished friend

CONTENTS

Foreword   5
Acknowledgments   7

BEFORE I SLEEP

I. Remembrance

Before I Sleep   15
Rememberings   19
E Pluribus: Eagle and Elm   21
Analogies   22
Theorem   23
March Thaw: Connecticut   24
Into Always   25
Hymn to Metaphor   26
Jape one   29
The Fact of Shore   30
Spring Leaf Burning   31
Equinox   32

II. Eleven Poems for November

The Pond   35
The Woods   36
The Brook   37
The Marsh   38
The Cape   39
Foretold   40
First Light   41
On Being Less Sure   42
Summer Cottage   43
Enough to Try   44
Reason   45

III. With Tongue and Cheek

Chromosonics   49
Ignis Fatuus   50
Open Letter   51

For Memory   53
Love Song for a Finch   54
Polemic   55
Christening in Darkness   56
Infallibility   57
The White Room   58
For Tomorrow   59
The Return   60
Defeat   61
Jeremiad   62
The Healer   63
Pedant   64
City '87   65

IV. Landscapes with Creatures

The Cry   69
Squall Line   70
Epithalamium Baroque   71
Vigil   72
Keep Us By   73
Canaan Mountain   74
River Man   76
Swans Rising   77
Three Cinquains   78
The Meadow   79
The Lipizzaner   80
Morning on the Square   81
Philohela Minor   82
Come Back   83
World Enough   85
Shared   86
Boy Lost   87
Seeds   88
For John Borg, Afterward   89
Salt Cay   90
Three Ravens   91

COUNTING I

Love Remembered	95
I Would Cry to Beauty	96
Paradox Enow: 21 May	97
Ponderosas	98
Leaving	99

COUNTING II

Waiting Snow: Connecticut	103
All Loveliness Can Be	104
Verging	105
Rest Fallow, Heart	106
Untitled	107
On Lines	108
For Yasuko	110
Harridan	111
A Song For Simple Things	112
Vesper	113

COUNTING III

Skylights

With Sky in All Directions	119
First Light	121
On the Burial of Shadows	123
Time Piece	129
Homage to Light	131

A Fish, a Frog, Two Birds, and a Butterfly

The Grayling	135
Concerto Scored for Spring	136
The Oystercatchers	137
Blue Mountain Lake	138
In May Returning	139

Longing and Leaving

My Love is All Around You	143

[11]

Walking Into the Wind   144
Let It Be Said   145
Knowing   146
Castle   147
Seventy Speaks   148
Cinquain Variations   149
Untitled   150
To An Estranged Lover   151
Enter October   152
Hymn to Orthodoxy   153
Now and Ago   154
Requiem With Five Graces   155

LOOKING INTO WOODS

Looking Into Woods   159
Dance of the Fiddlers   160
Downstream   161
In Praise of Sycamores   162
Inshore   164
Ministry   165
Anvil and Star   166
Another Time   167
Scale   168
The Double Dusk   169
Slower Than Waking   170
No Message   171
Chaos and I   172
Reflections   174
The Committee of Lesser Birds   175
Revel   176
First Light: Montauk Beach   177
Solution   178
Twelve: Thirty-One: Ninety-Nine   179
Northering   180

BEFORE I SLEEP

BEFORE I SLEEP

Across a meadow dim with stars
Two whippoorwills chant counterpoint
Harsh in this haze of August moon-hush:
BEFORE I SLEEP,
   Before I sleep,
      BEFORE I SLEEP,
        Before I sleep
They shout, and echo, as if to urge some
promised task
Be done now, before another night
Of unearned rest—some songs set down,
Perhaps, that haven't been,
Against a winter's doom.

I

REMEMBRANCE

for Robert Frost

REMEMBERINGS

I

The anvil of his mind is gone now, and his voice,
Gone off to some vast serenity of snow he
Loved so much. The verse will be around
A long, long time. It will have to be, for
It will take longer than that to let it be
Assayed. One thing's for truth; it won't be
In and out of style, like lace at the
Muse's throat. It will stick like burrs
To almost any mind it touches and like dock
Will spring in flinty pastures best.
Flint was his stone: from the hardness, sparks,
Sparks that lent no heat until, by undesign,
The waiting tinder smoked a wisp, and something
Burned.

II

Robert knew failure, lots of it, till he was
Almost old. Then suddenly he ran out of
Frustrations and got successful, just in time
For the Great War. By then he had enough
Wisdom binned to last till the Bomb—even beyond.
Things worked out, he said.

III

One sin was his forever talking, on and on
Like a brook that had got started down hill
And couldn't find much but rocks or drought to
Make it pause till it reached the pond above the mill,
Where the sun scooped it up, and threw it up
To the ridge again, to start over.

IV

What he was most was a teacher. Like
The needle, with only a prick of pain
He was into the inmost vein
Before you knew it, feeding disquiet
And wisdom straight to the main
Where they counted and held,
Unforgetting.

E PLURIBUS: EAGLE AND ELM
March, 1963

Three of the things that have made us *We*
Are a white-tailed bird and a wine-glass tree
And a sayer of poems not long left
To try for himself his cosmic heft.

Where we stand in the face of tax
And a dark array of fission facts
We think we know, and in knowing rise
To the morning's hint we may be wise.

These are the devils born of us,
And whether or not we like the fuss
We know that somewhere in the murk
They'll probably yield to harder work.

But when in our very birthright towns
The eagle and elm are forever down
And a friend is gone from an Amherst hill,
These gifts outright we cannot will

To come aright or come again
To tell us we are, and shall be, men.
Much can be read of our inward rift
In the way we stand up to loss or gift.

ANALOGIES

A neighbor ritual long ago agreed-to
Brought old Henderson sack in hand
Last Thursday to our willow swale to cut
His yearly right of saplings for the spiles.
He seemed to tell me—as if I couldn't read
The brittle nights and hatless days—that more
Was stirring in the wood than February
Knew, and soon I'd better take the hill
Road home to see. So I have come the long
Way out from town to know what maples in
The Cobble Bush are decked with pails, and which
Of those that chose the northern slope are
Winter-idled still by cold—if any is.

As ones not yet persuaded by analogy,
The Cobble maples now, like farmer
Women market-bound with wooden
Bucket-baskets empty, tell me tales.
I believe the one that says the sap that's from
The gnarled and northern trees is sweeter
Far for being late, and takes less fire
And stirring in the vats to thicken on
The stick.
                    It comforts me to see at least one tree
Is idle yet. This known, I turn my steps
Toward home, on yet another northern slope
Where, certain of analogy, I hear
Spring tell me never to despair.

THEOREM

October sunsets urge our hearts to peace
As maple gold gives back the summer sun
In gay oblation to a darkening world
To stay November's night. In autumn winds
The sky is laced with wavering skeins of geese
Whose calling, like the chink of silver chains,
Around the evening hush falls gently curled,
As saffron, scarlet, salmon fade to dun.

When sower's April and the harvest frost
Unite to tilt the agnostician's game,
So autumn and this season's falling gold,
Ignited by the alchemy of cold,
Will blaze again in ash and maple flame
To state that God is neither found nor lost.

MARCH THAW: CONNECTICUT

The tired house slavers.
Old snow slubs from the roofmoss,
Slides like diamonds down daggers
Along the bent eaves.
Spent clapboards curl with wet.
Doors lean,
Sills tilt and dribble while a season dies
From the attic down, racing into rills
Under the quilted meadow.
The white subsides to brooks that chime
Like bells of April peddlers in the hills.

INTO ALWAYS

On the round hill I sit and lean back.
Apple bark presses my spine, my skull.
I circle my shins.
It is cool in the noon lull of labor
In the round shadow of the tree,
Dark haven in a sea of the rolling sun.

I look out hard.
Today I will not accept horizon,
Nor any other imperfect geometry.
It was enough then, when I was old the first time.
No more.

I stare hard through the arches of my lids.
The circles of my eyes in the circle of my skull
Turn and roll,
And the round of my clenched arms wheels
As I spin tighter, tighter.
The horizon snaps and curls.

The small whirling orb of me arcs into always,
Over the crowsnests of the curving sea,
And the home of man flees beneath me.
I am at one with time and matter, where history dies
And there is no need for prophecy.
I journey the orbit of apples and stars.

HYMN TO METAPHOR

"What is darkness?" asked the Bat.
"I understand it has something to do with light,"
  replied the Sun, "whatever *that* is."

The problem of evil lies not in good, nor much less in
evil, but in our callow and persistent unwillingness to
accept the necessity of both.

If I were jesting a New Year in
(Or better an Age) with a proper din,
I'd cleverly hide in the gay debris
A wisdom word (from the likes of me!)
Regret would surely a portion be
Of a wise man's lore I'd leave for free,
And surely, surely some hope I'd dare
For all but the deedless debonair.
Humility's eyes I would favor there,
And love with a boundless heart to care:
But to certify the New Time in
I'd leave the latch-string out for Sin.

That sinning note is what troubles most
(As if Fun were somehow a burning roast)
So let us bend our necks together
To know if my theme will come to tether
In working mood, despite the weather,
And without the need for a lash of leather.
The sainted Word you've been waiting for
(Thank you, I've dozens of verses more)
Holds in its arms pale Wisdom's core
And's pronounced, by some, as Metaphor.
Poets, I hope, from the farthest coast
Will rush to my side to endorse the boast.

You may ask how a purely poetic device
Can illumine the nature of Virtue or Vice,
Or reveal to the glance of the lay enquirer
Which one, if either, is really the direr,
Or which is the mother and which the sirer,
Indeed the acquired, if not the acquirer.
Metaphor may in her figural guises
Lay an infinite clutch of potent surmises
Which hatch out as Science in livid disguises
Or dozens of similar dreary reprises.
I know that one sayer of fire and ice
Soon found it so useful he made it suffice.

One way to explain so beguiling a technic
Is to dress it all forth as the New Dialectic
(In spite of those longish though vulnerable leases
Of Hegel and Marx on their tired old theses)
And show that collisions of these with antitheses
Inevitably result in significant syntheses.
For it's twoness, not oneness, that generates newness,
As in marriages neither all loveless or rueless,
Or rooms with two windows not totally viewless
And mysteries baffling but never quite clueless.
(By now you may sense that my rhymes are eclectic
And the anapest pony's run off with my metric.)

So let us revere all the laws of duality,
Old Metaphor's soul, the well-spring of quality.
For tango-ing, two are the minirequirement
And likewise for loving, in youth or retirement,
In harmony, grieving, and relieving desirement,

Or knowing for sure what the bush-burning fire meant.
As in tenor and vehicle, the resultant of forces,
Our burnings together and cooling divorces,
The chords in our polkas and forks in our courses,
The triumphs of Error in Virtue's remorses—
Remember the dictate of Metaphorality:
That Purity's lovely *because* of Venality!

JAPE ONE

Few things I've heard of worse there are than
Jokes that go awry for being taken seriously.
Once the quip is lost, that's it—and one
Is stuck with having to limp the caper out as
Something neither fun nor meant.
                                        Eden saw it.
The jester Serpent *would* have his kind of sport
By testing Innocence to hear her twit
Him back on who knows what perception's all about,
Or how the heaven it was that sin got into apples
Anyway.
            She didn't twit. Right off she missed
The point that sin can't be unless there's fun
To fend against at least. And Adam,
Tired from the office, bought the line.
        So there's the risk the hasty jokester runs
Who doesn't count the human need for evil in:
A desert won, a splendid jape gone wrong,
A species lost to wisdom all these years.

THE FACT OF SHORE

There's no appealing from the fact of shore.
There land and water learn the strength of each.
The earth that's under whales slopes up to beach,
And prairies hark with hills to hear the roar.

A drier interelemental place
With somewhat less of sweep but more of guile,
The marriage bed, has been around awhile
And's done as much as shore to save the race.

These simple metaphors of beach and bed
Are Dialectic's theses met and wed.
Each says the law that we in mind must fix is
That which states that love is where the mix is!

SPRING LEAF BURNING

In April sun I go rake
The fallen gold of autumn time
(Sere, with feathered edge of rime,
The garden's stay against the cold)
A spice-blue incense now to make
Me earth-bereft and heaven-bold.
Strange how autumn maple smoke,
Or ash, or hickory, birch or oak,
Being labor-loved, is not for dreams.
Fall is a fact that can be told.
But April's leaf smoke always seems
To stretch the spirit, aching, taut,
Beyond and inward, far from aught
That spirit even hundredfold
Could ever say for wisdom's sake.

EQUINOX

The willows yearned for spring's own rain tonight,
But something in the moving air said no.
Now down along the gutter's cluttered flight
There cries a season's dark farewell of snow.

Silent the sodden snowflakes fail and drown
And merge in the shimmering pavement's sheen.
Only the mountain's curving foreland crown
And leeward ridges, the rain-black barns that lean,

Are white till morning light shall point the sea
And the saving wind bring blue to sky and lake.
Now, in my heartfall season's clamorous lee,
There's more than a dark or sunlit sky at stake,

More than a changeling snowflake's equinox
Of northering geese, the wind, or a questing fox.

II

ELEVEN POEMS FOR NOVEMBER

THE POND

Our pond locked up last night.
My morning glance turned back to ask
What had happened to the ripples,
And saw the far-shore pines up-ended
All in polished steel,
All pointing both ways, up
And down, like uncommitted
Arrows aimed aloft toward heaven
And at something downward
They thought they should suggest
But wouldn't state—
Some private legendry
Of rest below the skim
I wasn't entitled to at best,
But needed all the same—
So they surmised.
      How blest I'd be if I
Could pull a crystal sky down
Over me when things close in
And courage needs a silent time
To sort its warfares out
And guess on which it should
Be spent, from which withheld.
      The pond and I discern as one
That winter's will is wisdom's call—
If spring's to come this year at all, at all.

THE WOODS

Too wise to risk October's windrowed gold for snow
In one night's careless carnival of cold,
November woods are like to tell us early on
That there's still time for love:
Not only time, but we'd be better off
To take this snowless pause to mend our hearts
Against the day of ice,
Not to be out so for getting on to spring and June
At any cost.
              These waiting woods
Are gray as the tin of farmhouse roofs,
Steel dark, or grizzled as the flank
And muzzle of the whitetail buck
That lords the ridge. The granite stones
In unremembered walls, pieced out at pasture gates
With chestnut rails the hue of autumn haze
And silver barns, doze in lichen armor,
Waiting snow.

Such iron chiaroscuro glooms more somber still
For the gold of larches in the swamp, a gloss
Of laurel green below a birch, the sash
Of sumac, scarlet still, that warms
A sandy bank.

The woods are ready now.
One long night of starlit cold will see
The last leaf down and lashed for storm.

THE BROOK

I have not known many who would take
Noon to watch a November brook, even
From a sunned rock only a little cool
To the haunch. Such a brook is not
Like March or May, or any other season
One might love: there is never a lilt
Of rills or falls, even where stones loom
Or counter together at a turn to hiss
A brief denial to the downstream call.
Even though the sky is white, the water slides
Black as anvils, iron-hard and ringing
(You'd almost think) from a pebble tossed to make
The point. The ebon glint's a heaven shield,
And I've learned not to look for bottom when
A brook is thinking ice.
                          In all this glide
Of steel and hush there rides the burden of
A task undone, a task of snow and shadows
In the air, of otters in the night.
Such business is the brook's for now, as mine
Is mine. By choice we'll set communion by
Till June and work our winters out alone
Each in his own tried wisdom called, by some, design.

THE MARSH

Judging by birds I waded up them last few times
Out in the far slough mending blinds, they ought
To be a big flight through the marsh this year,
Once the weather starts to push. Lots of fledgling
Mallard in the timber now: you can tell them by the way
They lift their heads at rest—high and
Nervous-like. One time I clapped my hands, and
My God, they'd like to blew the trees down getting
Out of that pothole, straight up: next time,
They almost took my hat off flailing flat-out
Through the timber like a bunch of partridge
On a windfall apple drunk.
                                    They'll learn. Next fall,
Them that's left will come in high and later,
When the season's old, block shy, blind shy,
Shy of everything that moves or shines or makes a noise.
Can't say's I blame them. It's getting now, with warfare
Crouched on every reeded point, so most young drakes are
Cheated out of chance to make a circling pass
At painted hens and not lose more than feathers
From the tail: they're first-year fools—or else
They're feeders in the sundown corn who spend
Their days dead center in the sanctuary lake.
Too bad, I say, to lose the only years when
Sin and safety ought to mix. These yearlings who have
Learned to shun the gunner's magnum reach will have
To seek their memories up river in the spring.

But now, like I was saying, come Saturday I think
We'd better work the timber first, then later
Gun the slough. They's birds in there, I know.

THE CAPE

The last plover has cried and gone
Out over and along the woven pewter of my autumn sea.
The last summer wind has sung
The tilting water in to me
And flecked with spindrift gift
The land's last smile and the lithe sleepers' hands.
No sand devils dance like toy tornadoes
On the dune's far crest
To whisper showers to a waveless west.

The water moves, heavily,
From cloudline flat as lead
To gray beaches, level, with the hue of my dread
Season's sunless face.
The sad calligraphy of breakers
Curls my eye around the furling shore
To where, in lace,
The rip proclaims the time to take her rage
Between the spit and Point Hellebore.

A godwit tilts, then rides as fair
The tides of alien seas and lonely air.

FORETOLD

A mist of midges in a gather rise and fall,
Riding the pale November sun.
Silver webs, once looped in gingerbread
On peeling summer stoops, have battened now
The Season's last flailing
Dragon wings—are folded clean away
Like nets, no doubt in geometric cases,
Safe for May.

Oak and wheat await
The chipmunk's last quick excursion from the stone
Before the roar of snow,
And finches, chittering at a lockless gate,
Foretell the halo of the frost.
Things that have the wisdom-peace to wait,
Themselves cannot be lost.

FIRST LIGHT

Just west of tomorrow in the narrow
light of fading stars, just
now a fox, rust
on the amethyst snow, mousing:
     one more, he says, before sleep,
     cocking pricked ears for scurrysound
     under down.
From eastridge spruces watch,
all sawteeth and petticoats.

ON BEING LESS SURE

New England's wall, a skein of frozen stones
(Yankee buns I've heard them called in summer)
Cleaves the lonely upper pasture
At the crest, northeast-southwest,
Thrown like an arm across a sleeping
Lover's breast. It dozes now in winter's
Granite hold. Two days of windless snow
Have left no trace of stone or wall
To view. Lifeless the pasture hill
Lies waiting sun or April, hoping both.

With clearing comes a shouting cavalry
Of wind that eddies up wild dervishes
Of swirling silver smoke and peels
The wall's three feet of windward snow
Back to earth almost, save an inch
Or two—
              and there, where one would think
No life could be, lie broken to the light
Minoan labyrinths that fan away
In networks from the fortress wall,
Lanes where meadow voles have foraged,
Silent in the dimness under snow,
Or deer mice gossiped warm and safe,
For once, from stooping owls.

I say too sure we are, too often,
That things we take for true are Veritas
Unshakable. A snowdrift next a boulder
Wall, a golden glint in some far
Nameless galaxy—who knows what there
Of life may come to light when next
A clearing gale roars in? I'll wait and see.

SUMMER COTTAGE
Sankaty Head

The whale's earbone lies, a whorled Ahab fist
On the coffee table's blueglass sea,
A souvenir November-lost
In fragments of the locked-out noon.

Beyond the empty sun deck and the dunes
Old winds, as if through conchs and limpets,
Blow the slow green regiments of sea along.
Their white shakos roll with the curl
Of oceans lumbering always toward shores.

Through its white bone corridors convolute
The whale's ear speaks to no one in the house
Of soundings down the stairs of dark,
Of ponderous joys awash
In lulling hammocks of the dusk;
Of spume from arching flukes, the sheer shudder
And slap of unions vast as bundling moons,
And calves riding calm beside
Sleepy cows in the trundle swells of home,
Suckling.

The sounds of all seas fill
The sometime room as winter falls,
Slowly, to the scrimshaw mimicry
Of spiders in the failing light.

ENOUGH TO TRY

There's something a thrush is trying to say
In the gold of the year at the hush of day,
Something that's never found its word,
Something that could be sad or gay.

I've listened too much not to have heard
In the cry of wind and rain or bird
A something that's either love or a sigh,
A note that tells me it's wise to gird

For a test of hope when the moon is by.
The telling's to other than ear or eye.
The singer is doing his best I'd say,
And maybe, for once, it's enough to try.

REASON

Once, too hurt for love, in November
When grief sent me bitter
At sundown to watch Reason gutter
And fade, with only me to remember,
I lay in the cowling dayfall, falling
Into ashes with the light
Under the gray shawl of the late
Sky, and a far bird was calling.

The lone singing told me turn, and rise,
And look eastward to the new dark.
There, in the casual triumph of a star,
Undiminished rose my old surmise:
When mourning Reason, I must turn and mark
Her light some other way in dark, to keep me wise.

III

WITH TONGUE AND CHEEK

*Poems of Heresy, Humor, Terror, and Other
Norms of Reality*

CHROMOSONICS

Blue's a hue too pretty
    for the city. My bedtown maybe.
The cobalt stomp of thunder on
    my condominium becomes.

Yellow red's for town,
    uptown or down: the vermilion wail and shriek
    when succor threads a rush-hour street.

Now my neighbor, home gray from the Cacaphonium,
    shouts black trapezoids at toys on cluttered steps.
Cicadas etch green codas on a copper west.

Tomorrow lurks scarletly
    without: within,
    my platinum dialogues with ice and gin
    begin.

IGNIS FATUUS

I and a bittern cadge hope
From a yellow-lemon moon.
In the globed darkfall looming,
In the still reeds on the agate water
Of the heron's bog
A bittern booms his melon-oval tones
While godhead burns golden
In the marsh's womb, and the moon
Turns.

OPEN LETTER
1968

Write to me some time, College Man, some time later.
Do not write me now.
Do not try to communicate with me at all.

I am too busy to be serious,
Too busy to try to read your signs
Through the imposed veil of my hypocrisy and
Through the phony irrelevancies of my preaching,
Too busy feeding the GNP that gives
The leisure and the bread to mount
Your toy rebellions. My indignation is wearing raw,
And I have work to do.

If you must communicate, I suggest you address
The psychologists of your institution,
Or the social scientists,
Or perhaps the dean of the School of Education.
Their livelihood is to take you seriously, and to explain
To the elderly despoilers of your phony wasteland
The new wisdom of your liberation,
And the touching wholesomeness of your parietal urgings.
If they do not respond satisfactorily, there is always
The President, your pocket piece,
Who has learned how to live with you
(He's still President, isn't he) by learning
The motel business from the middle down.
Presidents, who have the highest salaries,
Are of course the first among the administration
To grow wise.

In any case, Son, there are a number of matters
Claiming what phony wisdom I can muster
At this time, and you may have heard

[51]

(Although there is no evidence to support that assumption)
What too many cooks do to the broth
(Broth is a kind of thin soup).

So forgive me if I seem preoccupied.
The thing you call the Gap is not all bad. Let's keep it wide
And deep until you have met a payroll once or twice,
Until you fail a time or two,
Until you in your callow bones know
The only real hypocrisy is humbleness gone slack
For lack of guts,
Until you know without our say that much
Phoniness is insecurity in uncommitted miniminds.

Write me later, after you are through
Baying at the chemist man
Who hunts your skills on salary in the spring.
Write me when the first chill serenity of
Reason's voice shall lift you wide-eyed up
In the calm of night.

You will know.
Write me then, if you write at all.
There may be work that both of us can do.

FOR MEMORY

For memory, now
Arias of elms in sleep, and
Owls feasting in a garden high with snow.
    (Hooked beaks click, scatter
    entrails
        and, after,
    half blinks of
    amber eyes
    slow
    and wise).

O sky, veined with elms naked, now
Sing me no memory. Charm me no
Owls trailing halos
In the snow.

LOVE SONG FOR A FINCH

The English sparrow doesn't dance.
He wears suspenders on his pants.
He's gray and brown and doesn't sing.
He's not much good at anything.
His taste in food is hardly chic.
His voice is shrill. He's far from meek.
He's held in finch esteem so low
I wonder why I love him so.
I think I love this guttersnipe,
This raucous, lowbrow archetype
Because, unlike his eagle rival,
I know he knows the game survival,
And I would like to learn from him
What war to bet my marbles in,
In what vacant lots to hide—
And why the lowly long abide.

POLEMIC

The bitter gist of headstones row
On row,
The dark anatomy of trees
On snow

Endorse as truth, the heroists
Among,
The sparrows' idiot senate in
The dung.

CHRISTENING IN DARKNESS

The Priest intones with shuttered eyes
The Glory and the Light,
While medieval cressets smoke
Against the gravid night.

The Glory and the Light, he chants,
Rise in the newborn cry.
The Lamb of God is lamb indeed—
The child we deify.

The Church's one foundation rests
On an infinity
Of souls to labor without end
In Rome's propinquity,

For Rome's infallibility
And pennies for the Rock,
That Rome may buy the will of God
To preach the boundless flock.

The bells and water sprinkled round
Complete the sinless rite.
The roar of Visigoths, their wolves
Unleashing, fills the night.

INFALLIBILITY

The Church of Rome still knelt to pray
Unfailingly the seventh day,
And donned with chanted stratagem
Old Peter's faultless diadem.

But then on Monday, just at dawn,
I saw an aproned ghost named John
Dusting in God's museum place
A minor niche for a dead ukase.

I asked him what the prospects were
For future sects that cannot err.
He winked and glanced aloft and smiled,
By silly questions unbeguiled.

THE WHITE ROOM
1918

From the iron bed where I lay
I watched them. No gore,
No severed tendons. Only the hands,
With enough wrist for credence, a man's,
Long fingered and sure.
They moved about the white room
Arranging the clear bottles, the enameled chairs.
They straightened a steel mirror on the white wall.

I thought, how competent they are, how quiet,
And how fortunate I am, soon they will come to me
And take my hands in theirs and
I shall know them. Certainly they have the skill
To do the other things hands were made for—
Point, clench, pray, strike, applaud, caress,
Express amazement or despair.
I longed for them.

They paused at the naked window,
Cranking the casement wide, then rested,
Fingers upright on the marble sill
As if pensive, waiting.
I reached out without rising or word.
They had ministered to everything in the room.
I waited, closing my eyes.

When I woke no hands were there, there
On the sill or anywhere,
Only two white birds on the marble ledge.
I watched the white birds fly
Out over white dunes, into the white sky.

FOR TOMORROW

By water wrought from the blazing air,
by ash from the tides of sand,
by patience from the hidden stone,

in the day of the shrike's caress
a cactus blooms lemon
and scarlet:

blooms alone for jerboa and burrowing owl,
for a silent moth,
for slow winds moaning in the charnel hour,
for tomorrow.

THE RETURN

I have tried to go back so many times,
Back to the smile of a golden season
Tanged with apple breath down-drifting
In the cool sundown from our gnarled orchard
On the hill.

Never quite arriving anywhere
I have tried to go back where
Glaze ice in cowprints on the ford banks
Told me something gold, and morning
    meadow wraiths
Spoke beagle music in the smoke
Of late September's amber afternoons.

But no, better the true tomorrow I can't escape:
And oh, how hard now
I have shut mind, eye, and how guarded
And stern I am against the marred going back,
The prevaricate return.

DEFEAT

The owl rides with hushed wings swift
To the forest shadows dark
Under a prickle of stars.
Alone he mourns to the night wood.
The hollow air throbs with his burden,
While jays and ravens cower
In a hemlock haven overhill.

From my dim window, toward the darkest hour,
White curtains grieve and wave surrender,
Belly softly to the west where
Night is crouched against the creeping lesion
Of the light.

JEREMIAD

How blind we grow,
Watching the idiot tempests come and go,
Oh, days on days
Until the senses' rigid embassies demur,
Until we lean and whisper,
"What did he say? Did he say
The mist was deepening? Did he say
There gloats above our Precinct's final tower
The pennoned skull we've loved against these ages gone?
And does the Matador of History mince and bow
At last with both our ears,
The tail, our trophy
Hooves?"

The accoutred mouse ascends the tree of birds,
Lance in teeth. Selah.

Ah, Delinquency of Grace, in our unvespered hour
Behold and bless: count not the silent books
Within our fecund lairs, nor sacred maps we've trained
To roll themselves back up at ages' ends:
          Rather kneel with us while velvet lemmings pause
At periodic shores to look, at least,
Back to where the mountains dream and stare
With temblors in their granite hearts
And snowbursts in their hair.

THE HEALER

"The snow arrived in our city at
long last during the night and left
it a veritable winter fairyland. . . ."

The Malden Courier, Nov. 16, 1914

Snow, last month's angel manure, rots,
The color of fall's gray bandage, windrowed deep
In after-Christmas parking lots.

Oh how it swirled bravely in to heal November's
  wounds
Under the neon's bloodless glow
So many carillons
Ago.

It will come again next year quiet
And white as doves or the new dead
To prove no rancor is, nor
Healing.

PEDANT

It is an uncomfortable barnyard fact
That the process of organic decomposition generates heat.
Farm boys do not wonder
At the steam that rises fragrantly
From the manure pile on nippy mornings.

Neither do they blanch, standing windward,
At the churning demonstration in a dead sheep's belly
Four days burst in the summer sun.

Many farm boys have been denied
The synthetic certainties of polity and the science social,
The fabricated festivals of faith and myth.
Most understand the visceral dialectic
Of ordure and chaos. There is a kind of
Serenity here.

Let us together strive to be that kind of farm boy
As we record the organic decomposition
Of our civic monoliths, our vested infallibilities,
Our benign universities,
Our venerable codes, our disciplined freedoms.
Let us not, unseemly, quail at the clog and stink
Of stacked humanity, the hype and
Hard rock of the motorcyle mentality,
The lethal pullulation of terroristic maggots
Doing their humorless thing,
The fake liberations of unreal bondsmen.

Let us with the farm boys be patient in our destined
Chores, trusting in the cleansing advent
Of the cataclysmic corrective and, someday,
Where the dead sheep lay,
The warm sway of marigolds.

CITY '87

Down the forsaken granite streets now walk the dead.
In silver silence they move from place to place,
An untombed host, with the slow doomed tread
Of sightless owls, or seraphs lately lost from grace.
The doorways speak no bread.

They have come here from a nameless town,
Forswearing holly and the gift of rain,
Warming themselves no longer in the scarlet gown
Of love, or courage, or the grace of pain.
They have watched the sky go down.

Cataracts of cloud tumble and surge
In silent silver from the chill slate of roofs,
Down the tall steeples, curling inward at the verge
Of praying doors from whose hands moves
A slow memory of doves and grief.
No grove, no bole, no bough, no vagrant leaf
Here greets the dead who watched the sky go down,
Breaking the trees in another town.

IV

LANDSCAPES WITH CREATURES

THE CRY

O Jessica
remember in the moon's last watch
at the hour before the tamaracks rose from the bog
under the shawl of morning
                    remember
the strange cry that fell whispering
down the velvet hills
                    the shudder
of air and leaves
and no wind but the sound of wings
passing after the cry
                    do you remember?
I cannot say what brought us to the wood
in the dark but the fear of not going
or the dim bell of a memory of earth
long sought in the wrong days

O Jessica remember
                    remember.

SQUALL LINE

Loose in a blue pasture of clouds
    wind runs burly like a puffing monk,
    buffets hawks up, up,
    tumbles crows straining home to the
        billowing roost.

Oh the push and nuzzle under the udders
    of clouds pendulous, the wild kiting
    of bust, buttock and belly
    of piled thunderheads coiling ponderous
    to gutteral drums!

Winds moan purple now, wail in a siren mode
    shouting track, track,
    and the dark in the sky
floods
down.

EPITHALAMIUM BAROQUE

Say whither, Ermine, imperial and most lissome Death,
Slim mesmerist of all hunters' moons,
Whither on what famished errand move
You now in this chill and venomed dusk? Is it to some
Hare dozing in a deserted burrow's nest
With only one door a stoat or bride must enter by
And go to find the moon again?
                                And
Will the first brushed leaf upstart the hare and
Knock her heart to send surging wild that blood
The narrow bridegroom seeks, and
Will he so deftly spring, embrace, and wait
With closed obsidian and patient eyes
Till beatings cease, and lust ebbs out,
And quiet comes while jugular and needles mate?

VIGIL

Come now, bend low
In our far dim wood.
Come see the elf runes
Of the Pilgrim in a dusk,
Where broken starfalls hum
A broken hymn, and wait to watch
A sullen moon come down.
　　Or kneel in the harbor nave
To praise the lightless ship
That slides the last time
Down the line of sky we called
Our dreaming's haven home.
　　Or this : go climb our hill in dark
And cup your ear and catch, if catch
you can, the lonely bells of
Martyrs, witches, principalities, emancipators, kings:
And while you're there, I ask you mark
Aloft the wheel of doves whose empty bills
Are plaintive for the sun.
　　Then come and wait with us
The night's long chill and vigil
Of our years.

KEEP US BY
A Litany for the Land

Oh Housatonuc, born in the ruck of one
Lost eon's granite jest that spilled your hills
From Gaylordsville to Canaan, keep us by.

When, rich with snows emboldened now in March by some
New urgency at river's end, you surge coiling down
Your bouldered way—yet seem to stay—Oh keep us by.

In April help us, with you, to lift our eyes
To hillsides stern with the hue of rock and iron,
But starred with tremulous bursts of shadblow white.

In the hour of curving trout, or August drought
When rivers show their bones: in October's flame,
Or winter's silent rest, Oh Housatonuc, keep us by.

In all days and seasons help us make our heart the land's,
To know the redeeming verity of mountain stream
In granite hills. Oh Housatonuc, keep us by,
Oh keep us by.

CANAAN MOUNTAIN

I have heard the work talk of crows at sunup.
From the Mountain's hickory flank and roost they loft,
Sculling the east wind's uphill lift, outward hoping
By two's and three's to the day's chancy gifts
Of corn or death.
                    The Mountain stays. It will be there
When sundown sends the sleepy toilers in, silent
Now for the dread of wakeful owls who else might mark
These westering ones for a raider's moonlit work.

The Mountain stays, too, for us, and is there for us,
At light and dusk, hunched toward Graylock's head.
Even our small journeys begin with a glance backward
And upward to the crest, a kind of touching of hearts
Before setting out for luck or loneliness.
In our dark or day returnings
Always the Mountain sees us home
To the southeast lee, safe again for rest.

Love and a mountain, call it. There are worse
Ways, worse things to lose a heart to now
When earth and we are out of sorts for hurt
That needs a long, long day to mend.
To know, the heart's hand leads us
By a granite stream green-gray with lichens,
Now down across a sugar bush through pasture pines
To Wangum Brook and tamaracks; then up
To hemlocks by the charcoal tender's slash that's healed
With maiden birch: to knob, cobble, and ledge, and
To table ridge where timber rattlers drink
A lemon sun in May, and greening marshes
Chant a vireo's song.

When our last long beckoning comes we'll beg
A truant hour for love. We'll go the steep side up

To Canaan Mountain, by Chancel Rock,
And, lo, be seen no more, not even for grief.

Our Mountain knows, and stays.

RIVER MAN

Sing him a song, O Sinnamahoning,
Sing him home, dead river man,
Lay him ashore in Conowingo,
Bury him deep with a jug in his hand.

Bury him deep, below Shamokin,
Away from the freshet, away on a hill.
Shout him a shout from Tuscarora,
Jig him a jig and a drunken reel.

Jig him a jig on Hummel's Wharf
When the last gray raft goes sliding by,
And the moonlit mist on the Susquehanna
Means logging water clear through May,

Logging water from Kittatinny,
And fiddlers twining the stars in grief
For a river man who left Duncannon
And evermore was the river's waif.

Sing him a song, O Sinnamahoning,
Sing him home, dead river man.
Lay him ashore in Conowingo,
Bury him deep with a jug in his hand.

SWANS RISING

From the hidden lake they labor rising, up in
    the early mist,
Their bronze voices calling, calling up the sun.
The white long wings sculpt, with thrust and lift,
The silver air and their trumpet echoes run

And clang like copper melodies along
The green-gray aspen groves below,
Telling the hills a day of song
May be in store—for those who care to know.

THREE CINQUAINS

MY CRAFT

My craft,
Like a jade falcon
Shut within a jalousie of willows,
Longs for your coming.
When will you come to me?

THE SPIDER

A pale spider,
Feigning satiety,
Yawns in his silver Theorem.
"How like opals glow your eyes!"
Observes the careless fly.

MY HEART

The slow tilt
Of hawks awheel
Over the shimmering arroyos
Weds my heart
To God.

THE MEADOW

The bullfrog lumps
Like a cool, peeled pear
In my curled hand
And,
He don't want to be there.

He unskins one leopardy
Propped up eye,
Winklike. He
Purdles. He
Grumples. And

BLIP!
He dives pondown,
Stoomping quick-kick to comfortmuck.

Moon will bear the bull's booming
(Lilting to lovers)
Later,
In the lilies of the water, or
In a meadow all silver
With melody and
Stars.

THE LIPIZZANER

Arched arabesques of grace,
Ponderous in lilting air the Lipizzaner
Rear and pirouette.

What hours the heart of patience tasked
These massive forms to poems
Lithe as swans aflight? What love
Beguiled the rippling flanks
To perfect step?

Hooved ballerinas move in cumbered unison
And kneel to end the dance.
In tanbark harmony of awe
The very ring applauds.

MORNING ON THE SQUARE
Venezia

In a grove of spittle and tablelegs
Two alabaster doves, down from the Campanile,
Strut, cock coral eyes at the fallen feast.
They worry a petal of artichoke,
Disturbing the peanut shells with pink toes.
Under the plastic privet
They moan the praise of tourists,
                                    and
With a snap and whistle of wings
They rise on a tide of sunlight
To patrol the casements of kings.

PHILOHELA MINOR

Out of the nomad sky, swift and alone in the
   harvest night
The woodcock drops,
Sideslips into the willow draw and down,
Safe home for now.
Each weary wing twice preened and folded neat
He sleeps, half journey done.

Cousin to curlew and phalarope,
Lonely, high-eyed waif with whistling wings
In the golden dusk of the year,
Long-billed voyager in the autumn dark
Whose paths are known by moons alone—

Can it be he of all birds who,
Lark-like in March, from giddy spirals
Shards of sunset music spills in twitters down the sky?
He trills his love, diminuendo, as he climbs.

The bride, leaf brown, is quiet in the grass.
Singing still, like a plunging stone
Her Cyrano descends and joins her in the dusk.

COME BACK
(1915)

Shore bird, sea child, ghost of the searching water,
Shy thing of dunes and the sweet marsh hay,
Come back, come home, O come, come stay,
Come back, O waif, in the brim of day.

   Between the slate of sky and sea there lies
   A salmon slash of sunrise low,
   Low along the Atlantic's eastern rim:
   Near in, spume high, fighting up the lines
   Of breakers on the crashing shore
   A curlew beats: then up, a-tilt, long legs a-dangle
   Down to the dune's lee grass at last he slides.

Shore bird, sea child, ghost of the searching water,
Shy thing of dunes and the sweet marsh hay,
Come back, come home, O come, come stay,
Come back, O waif, in the brim of day.

   High in the gaited winds of night
   How swift the etch of sickled wings
   When past the harvest moon you teemed,
   Golden plover, plover of the black breast:
   How many hearts of huntsmen rose
   To the piping wisp of gray against the east
   That spelled your coming in the dawn:
   And how many lonely beaches bore
   Brief trifid signatures that told
   Your comings there?

Shore bird, sea child, ghost of the searching water,
Shy thing of dunes and the sweet marsh hay,
Come back, come home, O come, come stay,
Come back, O waif, in the brim of day.

How many shores ago, young godwit, did gunners
Mark you skim the spindrift's edge
At Chincoteague and Accomac:
What startled lift of whimbrel watched you
Race the spume at Pamlico and Tuckerton,
At Montauk, Cobb, or Assawaman?
When knot and sanderling, when ruddy turnstone
Dowitcher, and avocet were more than names
At Barnegat and Manahawkin
And killdeer cried from the inland spring,
Who watched your flight from the wind-curved grass
We cannot know: so yearn we still,
From an alien time, to reach, and touch
Your loveliness.

Shore bird, sea child, waif of the searching water,
Shy ghost of dunes and the salt marsh hay,
Come back, come home, O come, come stay,
Wing low to the west, to the tumbling bay
And the heart's own shore in the brim of day.

WORLD ENOUGH

World enough is when the cricket vane
    to the wind's leaning
     swings,
         creaks,
and from the barn's loft haven
I peek through a halo of haydust motes
and float, float—I there adrift, lolling
in the June bales deliciously propped.

From this clover's Amen
    the cropped fields climb in my eye
    by lines of alders up a woodcock draw
    to skybend and
              around
                   as far
as the posts of the hayloft door,
but no further.

SHARED

Today I saw three doves together
Rise before a lissome nun,
Who, searching shamrocks in the heather,
Turned her back on the setting sun,

Turned her eastward softly singing,
And gently, as the evening failed,
She loosed and doffed her vestments clinging,
And gorse and dusk and me regaled—

Regaled us there without her knowing,
For not a word gave I, or nod.
Now once, at least, in sunset's glowing
I have shared a bit with God.

BOY LOST

The white helmets move back through the brush
To County M or O at the edge of farms,
Believing the bull horn.
The trembling dogs heel and cough
On choke-chain leash, too soon failed
In a romp, while, silo-sight away,
Under a blinking turret light a patient cop
Lulls the tired child a long day lost,
But lost no deeper into the prairie dusk
Than where the abandoned siding signal tower
Rose up, a castle.

> Up into the siding castle came the child.
> I, the ghostly signalman, was there. Together,
> Heads bowed over my feast of keys, we semaphored
> The yards of summer, calling up plumed cargoes
> (Oranges, armor, tigers, guns)
> Fit for any gandy dancer in the land.
> At our touch, down bright arrowed steel
> There swayed the red circus trains of April,
> Bound for everywhere, in jets of meteor light
> And cones of sound that aimed our hearts
> Across a prairie's rim to stars, or better.
> For us the four horizons rose and clapped their hands,
> Spilling a fist of golden miggies at our feet.
>
> But sleep you home now, lost boy who was,
> Sleep you now forlorn and safe from trains and dreams.
> At the siding castle's phantom tower
> My switchman's lights still flash
> The thundering Orient through
> But not for you, oh not for you.

SEEDS

The milkweed gift is silken cool,
And rides on wayward airs
With safety over dappled pool
And foals with silver mares.

A sterner seed in random loam
By bullock hoof is trod
To find in clodded dark a home,
And there consort with God.

In each the silent vestige sings
Of hope they may employ
When, waterless at darkening springs,
Our brothers we destroy.

FOR JOHN BORG, AFTERWARD

"For now flesh has let the gentle be called
Into the always—"

—From a contemporary Litany

I saw John Borg this morning at our bend
Of the Hollenbeck, near the fallen birch,
Stalking a rainbow trout. As he cast,
His line wove arabesques on the dappled light.

I shall see him again, in other summers,
Here in the mind's deft eye, casting.

Flesh is a fragile enigma that wears thin
And out, sometimes with no whisper to say
"It's time, I'm through." Traitor, if you will,
Keeper of pain that makes joy possible
And the twin gifts of passion and sleep,
Flesh makes us father, minister, player, ape.
Flesh goes in the end to a cold no snow ever said.
Let it go—with thanks and a little grief,
But not too much—
For when it is gone it is gone and will appear again
Only as flower and leaf, and we shall know it only
Alone and only in our marrow and in our dreams.

But the other, the John Borg who goes to no
Wintered earth, is locked in the blood of those
He loved or sired. In them and theirs his rectitude
Shall prosper, and in their bones shall thrive the wit,
Serenity, and loyalty that made his strength
The wisdom of a scholar's mind. Forever
Shall his love be borne on swallows' wings
And heard in the call of a thrush at dusk.

[89]

SALT CAY

Wind and spindrift and the swaying sea
Still move blue-green in a universe of sand and light.
Under the swells the brown bars
Stain the sky. At the reef,
Plumed suddenness of snow
Breaks, towers, and booms
To the inshore coral shelves coke-gray
And resolute.

Up island, hermits stitch the sand
Against the thieving wind.
Ground doves nod on the dunes.
A lone green heron owns low tide,
Sentry for the willet and the periwinkles.
Two bananaquits chip for our breakfast fruit.
Hibiscus nods. Days drown and merge.

THREE RAVENS

Frocked, hosed, and gaitered black like British vicars
In a country shire, eyes sharp for sin or scones,
Three friends, my crows, survey from leaning dogwoods
Elijah's window shelf of alms.

Within, I see them on the wall as ravens
Framed astride my family crest
(No lions, gauntlets, doves): SABLE,
ON A CHIEF OF GOLD, THREE RAVENS PROPER:
And, underneath, the Latin DEUS PASCIT CORVOS,
God feeds the ravens. So be it.

If I am to be the namesake of a bird
(The Normans say Corbeau but mean the same)
I'm glad I am the crow's. The crow is Time;
And crows it is that tell the patient man survival's
Not all strength and craft, but may be partly love.
The crows, not cocks, will caw man up to plant new corn
That dusty morning after he has burned
The sky down God's last time.

Elijah, at the window, plucks a crust of alms
And, standing tiptoe, gives the bread to each.

COUNTING: I

LOVE REMEMBERED

I know the silhouette of woods on sky at dark,
    the peace of shored whimbrels resting:
                            stillness
    at the nest of bedded lark
                        where air nor leaf
    stirs on the broken light
    of summer streams, their music hushed,
    all golden cowslips folded tight.

I share now the benign sleep of stones gray with stars:
    a serenity of wells and caverns
    whose mist drifts up at dusk
    from granite walls below:
                    the calm
    of sleeping farms,
    the dim embered sundown
    tolling an end to trespass in the heart,
    to weary eyes and arms,
    to love remembered.

I WOULD CRY TO BEAUTY

Time was I would beg to be spared the season
Of shadblow and trillium: to be shut
From the cool of meadows
In the luminous mist of the morning.
I would turn my gaze
From all loveliness,
The greengold coiling of fiddlehead ferns
In the dapple of birches at noon.
I would cry to Beauty,
"Be off, be gone!"

For this heart was at brim with an ecstasy
Flooding so bright that I foundered,
Gone drunk with the ache of satiety,
Closing my eyes to the wonder and press
Of it all.

And soon,
When the stun and the surfeit were eased
I would swear, like the drunkard,
To mend my way, and kneel
In the night of sobriety,
Certain of Beauty's return next day.

PARADOX ENOW:
21 May

This beauty's too much for a full season's holding,
Too heady a gift for a lifetime, or leisure.
One day at most in the summer's unfolding
Could anywise hold such a boundless measure.

And a day is enough to savor perfection
(If love is sufficient for days with rain.)
Too much of anything calls for discretion
Save poems, and passion, and pardon, and pain.

PONDEROSAS

The ponderosas fondle the wind with whispers,
Sifting the faint mist softly,
Swaying a little, like saints saying matins.

I stand as straight as they, under them,
Looking up wonder-tall through the light,
Catching the prismed sun shafting down in the gloom
Flecking warmth on my upturned face,
Gold on the aisled earth around me.

Pines, big ones, loblollies, sequoias,
Flock slope and field, combed up
From the land of Oregon or Georgia:
Shed windrows of calm,
Even reason,
On the tilted face listening tight-eyed
To a music of peace wrought new
From a jumble of broken moons.

LEAVING

Swift as the lash of an otter's eye
Quick ruffles flash on the pond's
White sky, tiny shudders of air
Fanning out to nowhere. The waters
Flicker and ripple, subside,
Then die to glass,
To silence.
              But they have said something,
These moving whispers of wilder weather
On the way.

Loons and grebes, reading air, restless,
Wake early at morrow for a last minnow
Before running on the water,
Lifting off,
Leaving.
          Northwest,
Real waves rumple the lakes,
Fling white flecks
At granite shores.

COUNTING: II

WAITING SNOW: CONNECTICUT

At Saybrook the dune's gray grass bends
Landward. The town's last willow leaf is down,
And a white spire broods the hour.

Up country among the deliberate hills of Cornwall
The torches of tamarack gold have guttered
And fallen, needles strewn on the marsh.
The rivers are lidded with ice—
Black paths for gull or star they are—
And in the sinuous valleys their unseen waters
Lip the secret shores beneath.
Darkly they slink among stones, truckle and slide
Seaward in their narrow lanes,
Purling under agate roofs no matter
When the snow comes whispering,
Or a black bell tolls in the steeple.

ALL LOVELINESS CAN BE

All loveliness can be
In aspen leaves.
Ask one who has seen, ask
One who now in the sunless wood
Of blindness once touched, once knew
In a last, lost time
The shaking of golden hearts
In a grove gray-green at noon
Before snow,
Below the exponential granite
Of Loveland,
           Royal Gorge,
              Red Mountain,
                 Tennessee,
                    Berthoud,
                       Independence.
In aspen leaves
All loveliness can be.

VERGING

I wander in tidal eternity,
A voyager windheeled or adrift
On the lifting breasts of the sea,
My prow cleaving time, light,
And the unhurried, implacable water.
My seamless history unfolds and merges
To shadow behind me as I go.

I, traceless and alone,
Move without mission toward headland havens
Which do not exist, verging always
But never quite beaching on the lobed
Sands of sleep, or home.

For I the alien seeker drift, locked in the laws
Of sea and flesh, furled in a dim infinitude
Of twining helices, lodestars, edicts of genesis
And homiletics now and forever and ever.

Insubstantial wanderer of time and water,
Argonaut and verger to the light,
I am the lost and trivial helmsman
Of the night.

REST FALLOW, HEART

Rest fallow, Heart, though in cold you're grieving.
The winter dark is long and does not yield.
The autumn's plow and harrow now are idled,
And rime lies white upon your broken field.
Be silent, Heart, in hurt and yearning.
Lie still while frost and root embrace.
Let no song mar your darkling sojourn there,
No velvet gift, nor crown of bridal lace.
Seek patience, Heart, in travail trusting.
The winds of spring someday will gently blow.
The seeds of love are not too deep for greening,
But must go down to winter's earth to know.
Wake singing, Heart, at last in May rejoicing.
Like winter wheat you've earned your gift in grief.
Rise up serene in love and exaltation,
Now wiser, nourished, richer far in seed and sheaf.

UNTITLED

Trellis well thy heart, my dear,
With spikèd vines and sweet.
Both beautify and fend it well
For love is strong, but love is fleet.

Then sit within thy heart, my dear,
And vex the passerby
With words of wisdom set with thorns
And yearning, downcast eye.
Do thou this, and so shall I.

ON LINES

"But what is this true form of art? . . . Here's how I
realize it. I employ no other line than the curve,
which possesses freshness and force. I compose these
curves so as to bring them in accord or in opposition
to one another. In that way I obtain the life of form,
i.e. harmony."

ELIE NADELMAN

Ben called from the yard, "Come see.
There's a rainbow." I went and we stood in the open,
Away from the dripping maple, looking up
At the misty benediction that curved
Like a pastel ribbon against the purple bruise
Of the retreating storm.
                                    The blessing didn't last;
As we watched, it evanesced
Into the rain-fresh light. It was almost
As if it had come to make shy amends
For the noon's dark turmoil in our hills,
The storm we could still hear mumbling doom
To the valley farms southeast of Sharon.

Later, after supper, on the porch, Ben fell
To talking about lines (of all things) and what
They mean, or seem to mean. He has a touch
Too much poet in him to shrug a glimpse of beauty off,
And I could tell the rainbow had set him
Mooning. He said, assertively enough
To make me turn my head, "There are only
Two kinds of lines, you know—straight and curved."
He paused to see whether I would stay or
Remember the unwashed dishes.
                                    "And so?" I said.
He went on. "Straight lines frighten me.
Don't they you? I mean we never, we can't
Know where they really begin, and certainly

[108]

We don't know where they end, any of them,
Like eternity. The only thing we can do with them
Is to pretend to break them, and use the pieces
For triangles and squares and such, or measure
With them. The air is full of them, unseen,
Like minutes and hours and years—and all we can do
With *them*, too, is to use them for measures,
Then watch them go, like the rainbow.
Who ever held on to something that has no beginning
And no end, and felt for sure that it was his?
It terrifies me, not knowing where something has been
Or where it's bound."
                        He put his hand on mine
And his voice softened. "Curved lines don't do that.
I feel comfortable with lines that seem as if
They might come back to me, or ones that have,
Like your arms around me as we fall asleep.
Now that rainbow today: it wouldn't take much
To make me believe it curved full circle, down
Into the earth and up, and for a moment
Linked the sky and land together
As surely God intended. His hand I know
Made halos, wedding bands, and all our other
Small horizons. Neither they nor the
Warm sweet curves of your breast and thigh
Take my eye straight off to nowhere
As straight lines do. Remember, too, the year
We flung a crew out toward the moon and found
No star with points at all—all round as suns
And bocci balls."
                        He caught me nodding off.
"I'm sorry I lulled you down again to doze.
I shouldn't go on so about things
That make no difference."
                        We rose, hand in hand,
And started up the spiral stairway all the neighbors
Envied, circling slowly up to dreams.

[109]

FOR YASUKO

Y	E	L	W	A	Y
A	Y	I	O	N	A
S	E	K	R	D	S
U	S	E	D		U
K			S	B	K
O	T	S		E	O
!	H	H	T	G	!
	A	A	H	U	
	T	D	A	I	
		B	T	L	
	S	L		E	
	M	O	L	▲	
	I	W	I		
	L		L		
	E	O	T		
		N			
			T		
		T	O		
		H			
		E	H		
			A		
		H	N		
		I	D		
		L	S		
		L			
		S	T		
			H		
		O	A		
		F	T		
		S	S		
		P	I		
		R	N		
		I	G		
		N			
		G			
		▲			

HARRIDAN

You're not much of a month, March,
You charwoman. A broomstick harridan, I'd say:
Howls, deception, sleet, tears—
A ruddy bitch of a red-nosed nuisance you are
With your yea's, nay's and maybe's.
Not many trust you
But crocus and snowdrop and woodpussy cabbage,
Or those swaying boas of willow gold—
And always the credulous buds of the maples
You lure in a sunburst
Then lunge at with iceteeth and whiplash
While their sweet clear blood rises
To spile and pail.
                    So now, sloplady
Of the third month, now that you've scoured
My brookbed with freshet
And pruned my sugarbush maples with bluster
And snap, harassed two cowering
Great horned owlets high in their stricken
Sycamore's swaying loft—
                        Leave!
Leave if you please while the north wood is calling
And a dryad named April
Is whispering near.

A SONG FOR SIMPLE THINGS

I have a heart for small and gentle things—
First star: far steeple on a gathered town:
A need for separateness to heed a circling hawk,
Or know an owl's last low and sleepy tremolo
Before the slow line of sun slides down the hills
To brighten golden boulders in a brook.
    I am in love with simple, lovely things.

I've hungered long for shy and hidden things—
The plunging woodcock's amorous trilling from the sky,
A dazzle-sheen on beetle wing beneath the bark:
Foxfire in a rotten stump I scatter with a stick,
Or cooling kiss of milkweed silk along my cheek:
The pepper-tingle of nasturtium greens I bite.
    I am in love with hidden, simple things.

VESPER

The sun, just now dying:

Now gone, beyond the wood behind my lake,
Down in double glory, rose and amber—
And only one thin long wedge of black
Between the waning lake and sky:

Now silence, windless and pure,
And purer still for a thrush's silver elegy,
Woodwind sweet and clear in dark,
On lake, on sky.

COUNTING: III

SKY LIGHTS

WITH SKY IN ALL DIRECTIONS
For Freeman Dyson

Driving north I pass the clean geometries
Of winter cordwood: salt-killed maple, hickory,
Ash, stacked in the yards of autumn farms
On the guardian hills southeast of Shelburne.
Soon a cold topology of snow
Will fold around them, on them, round them off
Into a landscape lost to white.

This soft conceit persuades me, once for all,
The world I knew has slipped the bonds of old
Dimension. It leads my liberated senses back
From log to tree to seed to genesis,
Where nothing was but energy, or God:
Beyond and down to matter yet unseen
But still perceived: perhaps to light itself,
First known by Gaia's eyes in that one hot,
Eternal macrospark before the realms
Of space and time began.
                                                And then the snow !
Janus-like, I feel my visions merge
From east and west to north and south, from
One-ness somewhere at the atom's riven heart
To the vast diversity of snowy flakes
And all they do to cordwood and to hills.
As if eyes were not enough, I hear infinity

Afoot within a flaring universe
Of moons and hurtling ruck, a diapasoned
Harmony of energy and mass and speed,
The sigh of curving starlight verging toward
And merging in the wondering eyes of men.

Now my earth, with sky in all directions,
Holds all I'll risk of new awareness,

Enough of unified or diverse Godhead
To strain old Hegel's dialectic web,
The metaphor of Frost, the legacy of sin
In Eden's gift.
                    For peace or rage, fresh ways
Of seeing snow and cordwood of a sudden
Measure me in new and sober ways.
I now look in and out around the compass,
Up to new infinities—and see
The eye of Order peering back. So I no
Longer count my waning days reluctant,
But walk the meadows of humility
At evening, counting stars.

FIRST LIGHT
(*Gaia Speaks*)

Two, maybe three moonscapes ago,
From out there, further out than even now
You can imagine, I heard a celestial click. Afterward
There was a pause—not long, a millennium
Or two perhaps—before it all happened.
                                        Then,
THEN there was a Bang, big, bigger
Than all but the First One. I felt a rush
Of velvet dust against my face. I knew the smell
Of burning stone. Clearly there had been
A beginning of something.
                            And suddenly,
Warm on my cheek, my virgin eyes,
The New Thing, moving in a whisper of air:
Light had happened—
                        and with it came a sound,
A new sound clear and sweet all around me,
A golden singing of flutes and the bells of seraphim
In the first dawn.

ON THE BURIAL OF SHADOWS

AN OPEN LETTER

TO

STEPHEN HAWKING

Who Would Ride the Winds of Metaphor
To the Farthest Reaches of
Poetry and Knowing
even
Unto the Ultimate Realm of Beauy,
Which is Light.

I want to tell you something, Stephen:
You have rattled my kaleidoscope long enough.
It is my turn, an aging reductionist
On this hurtling cinder, once again to train
My dialectic on the elusive formulae
Of reality: my turn to try at least
(Mind you, with that bardic double vision
Known as metaphor) to wrestle down reality
To a solemn new equation for the press.
Poetic laws forbid a poet's try at proof,
So tremble not. Just post what follows
On your chalkboard, as together we await
The latest chariot of starlight's swift arrival
At our shared sill of darkness.

$$L = \frac{E}{B^3RM^2}$$

Let L be light, and E eternity, while
B is beauty to the power of three, times R
For reason, times M for mercy squared.
When I am through enlightening you,
I shall leave this formulaic masterwork
To you for your judicious explication.
Meanwhile, hear me out in my humility.
In the frolic of my sunset years two things
Bewitch me sorely, as they do you in youth—
The fact of time and the mystery of light.
The first I have exorcised, tamed, and in
My wisdom laid to rest in the comfortable
Shroud of metaphor. The second has proved more
Troublesome, in fact elusive. Wordsmithing
Fails; the old sleight of tongue garbles,
Chokes, boggles; but on I go undaunted.
Observe, my friend, this double clutch from Wisdom's
Craggy nest—

"What is darkness?" asked the Bat.
"I think it has something to do with light,"
Replied the Sun, "whatever that is."

I once asked my grandson why he
So earnestly dug in his sandpile.
"I am burying my shadow," he replied,
And cheerily returned to his task.

II

When the last star gutters and fails
And the moons in the void go black:
When the condor sleeps in our garden of trolls,
Sleeping the shallow sleep of husks and moonset:
When butterflies howl and kestrels slide
Down the last winds, and the anaconda
Coils in the hummingbird's nest: then
Shall we waken in the old ossuary,
Chanting new epitaphs for Reason, Reason
That yet roils and heaves like magma underfoot,
Seeking fissure, seeking the light which
Is no more: then the masque of twilight
Will be done, eternity turned sour
In the sycamore seed. In a gray nimbus
Of farewells Ra will subside to sand
Again, sceptreless, and Aurora will flicker
And exit in tatters.

                    But Blake says one tiger
Burns brightly still, and in the nurseries
At sundown old nannies croon, "Mica, mica,
Parva stella," while half a world away,
After the great light at Hiroshima, in the
Silence of ashes two lasses talk of men
And the bounds of knowing. Pandora weeps,
And Eve looks sadly out upon the
Latest garden brought to grief:

"Omnia scire mori est, omnia scire,
Apocalypsis nova—"

        And if you would know
Light as apocalypse, be in Oklahoma
Mid-May when the writhing line storms
Detonate the earth with terror's coiling lash
And only the mountains hold fast in the
Rape of land under a cowering sun.
Go to earth. Take cover.
Do not speak.

        Or if you would know light
As affirmation, be atop Katahdin before
Sunup on a clear June morning, alone,
Looking east. Watch the new light
Arrive on your continent. Do not speak
Until you are down and
Back in town.

        For between affirmation
And apocalypse looms our craven shield
Against the gifts of dark and light,
And we shall lie down in one and rise
In the other as if the infinities
Were birthright and pocketpiece.
Always in tremulous passage, we do not
Linger, but the time of light is
Always and always.

III

        Now again the Bat speaks
And the Sun answers, and neither knows
Wave or quantum. And I, Stephen, applaud
You, as my grandson in you seeks to bury
The shadow of our unknowing in the
Tranquil field of unity: to codify our gravities,
Even unto the dark vortices which one day

[126]

May devour all we've learned of beauty,
Compressing stars into the adamantine birth
Of universes yet unknown, unseen,
Free, for once, from deity and sin.

                              But before
My humble close, I'd make assignment, homework
If you will, as from a caring teacher:
Read once more Books I and II of Milton's
Noble chiaroscuro stay against the thief of light,
The sonorous epic of a garden lost to grace.
Go with Arnold to the beach at Dover and look
In moonlight south to France. Close your eyes
And hear the light of Spirit sing for Blake.
Then know the terror of an empty street
As Frost's gaunt luminary clock proclaims
The void of time against a dark and lonely sky.
Renew once more the tales of Daedalus, Hyperion,
And Mother Gaia in the dawn; and in another
Dawn go back to Stonehenge as Hardy's Tess
Lay sleeping after flight, all unknowing that
She lay upon the sacrificial stone: that soon
The dagger sun would pierce the sacred
Cleft and show the sheriffs to their prey.
And finally, spend a humbling hour
With Meredith and seek the dusty answer
Waiting there for those who beg for certainty
At any cost.

IV

And so, my bright Enquirer,
Press the search as only you and yours can
Press it in this dizzy spate of magnitude,
Velocity, and hope that swirls about us all.
Take some care lest your quarks and photons
Tumble down the jaunty rabbit's hole and frisk

With Alice and her founding mathematician's
Whimsy in a dream. Beware!

                        I'd ask you last to
Know at heart that Beauty is our common way,
Yours in primal ultimates of mind and space,
Mine in gratitude for each new day, in knowing
That the light is here. For light is really all, I think:
All things begin and have their being here where
Mother Gaia first conceived and had the word
From God, and gave the earth to light.

                             Don't range
So far we lose you. Take a little time to do
Your homework, remembering our affection
For the bright geometry of our old kaleidoscopes
That do not work in dark. From Starlight,
Make us new serenity. From the new Chaos, make
Us love. From Time, a shining garland
For our journey's close. From all you find beyond,
A charm of Beauty crowned with Reason
And with Light.

                Carry on—

TIME PIECE

(For Cronus)

"I saw eternity the other night
Like a great ring of pure and endless light."

HENRY VAUGHAN

Time?
Time, Sir, is the flow of swansdown blown
Too high in the wind's realm for us to know,
Moving without percussion or fuss to the rims
Of everywhere as it animates the clever metronomes
We've made to mark it pass. Laving star
And sphere, it flows ceaselessly among the firmaments,
At one with the luminiferous ether.
There are no pausings for madrigals or remembrance:
It is all business, and we, we are lost
In its tender inscrutable bustle.
Our whimpers and wonderment unsaid,
We linger in its litter of yesterdays.

Or this: in the sea-distance, Time is a
Tempo of dolphins stitching the loomed water,
Without effort emerging in arcs sleek with silence
And entering again that water, endlessly
Sewing sea to sky in a glory of wholeness.

Hosannas struggle unsung in our throats,
Each in his own perturbation yearning; for
Over the shoulders of learned tinkerers we have peered,
And in a sputter of revelation seen gravities unknown
And the bending of light as dying stars rush
To the cold vortices of oblivion. We have stroked
The patient hoopsnake who eats his tail, and debated
New modes of periodicity as we peeled the onion
Of eternity.

We have, in short, strolled the future and,
Trembling, watched the past come plodding on.
We need no longer fret, knowing that Now
Does not exist: that Time remains at
Best a flimsy line of credit: that
All our tinsel altars still must serve.
If there is to be or ever was a beginning,
And if there was or is to be an end to it all,
I fear we shall not know it, even so.
Or if, in a burst of starlight
Shards of shattering glaciers cleave the falling air
And all shall cease, then so be it: at least
We shall have tried the old obsidian gates
Of Cronus, failing all.
                        Better we go to earth
Again and join our mentor Fox. There
In havens old we may reflect with gentler
Hope upon the darkling truth above.

HOMAGE TO LIGHT

To the Memory of Arnold Whitridge
29 January, 1989

> The learned ones do not know light,
> seeking its nature in the sterile void and blather
> of numbers. It is not to be found there. It is
> everywhere else. It *is* everything else,
> all matter and force, even in darkness,
> without which we could not know it,
> we and the moon.
>
> —ATTRIBUTED TO ST. SEAMUS OF KELLS

And so, Seamus, we know light, you and I,
As Aurora borne on white ravens' wings
At the day's beginning. Or better this—as
The golden flagship of infinity,
Bright voyager of the Cosmos, ethereal and swift:
Or Beauty in her luminous guise, that old Divinity
New clad each year in April's willow gold.

At evening when our mother star, the Sun,
Rides down beyond the skyline, renewing hope
To brotherlands below, she leaves her wraith
As keepsake in the moon and in the glowing
Embers of the hearth to mark her sure return.

New light, we know, is crouched alert in matchtips,
And rides within the sperm whale's brow at sea:
For light is passion and the gift of sight
And sentience, the spurt of struck flint
In the dry grass, the lurk of magma under earth.

We know that light is not
The lonely toll of steeple bells alone,
But the chime and tingling melody of all
Bells: the crackle of blue glaciers breaking:
The song of sunlight spilled on prairie snow—

[131]

All ambient webs of sound made visible by joy.

In the drift of silver mist on Dingle Bay,
Or over the purple reach where Tagus feeds the sea,
I hear the ticking of each numbered day
When torch or sunlight sees a coffin down
To silence and the old forgotten solace of the clay.
But even there the light is always ours to know,
For love and ash are gift to fields where roses blow.

A FISH, A FROG, TWO BIRDS
AND A BUTTERFLY

THE GRAYLING

In leaps twisting up,
Out of the swift riffle the grayling
Skitters, flails to snap the silver gossamer
That urges him against will, current, the alien air.
Fins lash, all lavender sheen and
Green stipple.
                    The barb prick stings now.
Soon, all lunging done, he slides side up
Into the soft entrapment's
Waiting web.

CONCERTO SCORED FOR SPRING

There's nothing new in Hyla song.
It's all been sung before.
No April snowfall's ever strong
Enough to quell that joyful score.

The tiny pent-up tympani we hear
Trilling ecstasy to star and earth
Remind us all, at each new greening year,
What winter's fragile death in song is worth.

THE OYSTERCATCHERS
For Martin and Cindy

It was just before feeding-light one morning
On the beach at Ocracoke when I saw them,
A slow folio of four oystercatchers
Winnowing the golden air, making sleepy trumpet talk
As they flew north along the dune crests.
I like to think they'd roosted, heads tucked,
Ankle-deep in the tiny surf of the lee shore, belonging.

I followed them against the early sky.
They dropped away, two into a sand flat to the west,
Two onto a stubborn gravel bar the incoming tide
Was already hissing at.

How beautiful they were, black on white against
The pleating water, orange bills stitching the shallows.
True to their ancient commitment
They probed the shelled bounty, taking what was there
For them without wonder or guile,
That the web be not broken.

BLUE MOUNTAIN LAKE
(*Adirondacks*)

An April wind slid over the flat lake all
    moonpocked and honeycombed
    in tin tones.
             Breakup time.
Chill still, the sleeping water waited, patient
    for blue and the soft nestle
    of mallard breasts come May: and
    the wind,
          the wind
    lost itself in the hills.

IN MAY RETURNING

The monarchs, tigereyed in the goldenrod,
flicker and glide, russet kites
tether-loosed at the sun:
ricepaper wings hover
among hollyhocks, browse clover
in the drowsy meadows of September.

One twitches away, flips downbreeze: skims
back up, lights: curls
hooked legs round a saffron sepal: tilts,
outflings the watchspring tongue: steals
nectar: rises in the lavender morning,
laden for journey.

Sunchild, windmote, off soon at noonstroke
to Mexico somewhere, down
the boisterous air voyaging:

Fly strong and safe there, you fragile testament of Love,
you incredible Darling, my Godhope, my Beauty,
as safely in May returning,
returning.

LONGING AND LEAVING

MY LOVE IS ALL AROUND YOU

For My Wife, Florie,
On Our Fiftieth New Year's Day Together

May angel fingers close your eyes tonight,
And starlight soft surround you,
Three robins tell you true, at waking light,
My love is all around you.

And through the day, 'til sundown steals my sight,
I'll praise the day I found you,
And tell you true myself, in words still bright,
My love is all around you.

WALKING INTO THE WIND

I have walked into wind in winter,
    the push, pummel, and pause of it
    breaking my step sometimes.
    I have loved the whish and whistle of it
    tingling in my ears, my fingers.
    My long scarf ripples out.

Once I hid behind a tree to make it find me, and
    it laughed when it did, and then
    I backed into it a step or two
    (to stop the cheek-sting and
    draw a mitten across my nose, for decency).
    All right, all right, I shouted
    when it blustered me again and
    threw its arms around me so strong I
    skipped a breath. I leaned hard into the wind then,
    my head down sideways.

It's a kind of joy to walk against a strength like that
    and no one hurt or even meaning
    harm, just assertion, as in a strong
    marriage.

LET IT BE SAID

Let me be one who is after known,
In words on wood or simple stone,
As one who in the anvil's form
Saw Reason reign and Beauty born:
Logic stripped to line as pure
As usefulness and purpose sure
Can ever come to Euclid's dream
Of Beauty bare, of Form pristine.

And I've also learned from three score years
(Plus twelve or so—and some valid tears)
That Truth can best be brought to birth
By working *down* from Heaven to earth
Toward Socrates' old one-on-one,
And certitude not given but won—
The kind of peace that Beauty brings
To those who heed the useful things.

KNOWING

The clasp of lovers twining,
Now soaring wind-free, flesh bereft,
Now taming the slope of summer field
With the sweet locked thrust
Of flesh.
       Then, at day-dim,
Sun failed down the west,
Breath at brim, slow the cool stretch
Of thighs on moss, again, again,
Only the shadowed stream brink knowing.

At last ceased, eyes half eased,
Ears dumb as the stilled drone of day sounds,
Two, as one,
Slowly become the night.

CASTLE

1933

For many careless hours we toiled
    There on the beach,
Patted and shaped a castle royal
    Of sand, and each
    Visioned it done.

Heedless of the tide's dull rumbling
    Still we pelted,
But at last it caught us, humbling
    Castle, melted
    Now and fallen.

We laughed and tried to understand,
Viewing the ruins hand in hand,
    Why we hadn't thought
    About the sea.

We built one later, though,
    In a higher place
And barricaded it so
    That it is still safe
    From the tide.

SEVENTY SPEAKS

Days in youth are not for counting.
No wondering, then, the number left to spend,
Or why, or when, or whether any's worth
A try to keep against a future's end.

Now I have found at last that days in age
Are not by any sophist's bend of truth
For us alone, and will be repossessed.
No day is ever ours. No noon, no span of hours
Belongs: when spent, each must return to grace
A newborn's fragile gift of breath, and thus
Keep true the iron link of birth to death.

And so, each night between my dark and sleep,
Gratitude and praise for beauty said,
I take, as is my heart's quaint custom then,
The day just gone, fold it flag-like
As soldiers do for fallen friends, render
It to Heaven's outstretched hands, and turn
To rest.

CINQUAIN VARIATIONS

SOUNDS OF APRIL

Jonquil
Hearts sing golden
Songs when April broods the
Hills and green anew the woodland wears.
Hylas
Chanting
In the marshes
Tell us winter's lost its
Heart to tadpoles, shadblow, tulips,
Godspell.

THE WHITE TULIP

A white tulip
At evening nods, drops its petals one
By one into the silver night. A jealous
Moon secretly marks where
They fall.

GEORGIA SUMMER

A cicada
Sutures the humid air with a
Needle of sound. The butterfly is still.
Desire swoons as day loses itself
Among the vines of evening.

[149]

UNTITLED

Death for my grandfather
    came slowly, as sleep in prison comes,
    came gently, as hills diminish
    when dark and dew let down
    and breath flickers to silence.

There is quiet enough for all time
    in the stilled hands of one old man,
    in the quelling chill of twilight
    in his eyes.

TO AN ESTRANGED LOVER
(Remembering Edna Millay)

The last train for twilight will await
Me at some lonely star-emblazoned gate
    My lost tomorrow.

I shall be wiser then. No fear of fate,
No scarring from an uncoiled hiss of hate,
    No trove of sorrow

Will hinder me, nor make the journey long.
Dark winds will pipe me there for want of song
    To buy or borrow.

So seek me not with kiss or dare, my Dear,
For stilled is the reckless heart that withers there
    In house so narrow.

ENTER OCTOBER

For my wife Florie

Today begins the Masque of October, month of
Bright death here in our hills: the rollick
Of leaves blowing, the profligate falling, the scarlet shout
Amid the ancient carnival of transfiguration.

Low stars watch as the moon, swollen with gold
Of corn and pumpkins, lobs itself
Over the far hills into the blue steel
Of still air keen with frost.

It is September that dies a drab: leaves hang
Listless and sallow with a summer's dust,
Drooping and spent.
                  But October it is that tingles
And sings in a blue heaven of bonfires,
Of skim ice at sunup, the sowing of love and leaves
In this sham death of regeneration.

So rollick anew, our own October!
Blaze away! Blow your shrill trumpets
Of dazzle and tree-song, you leaves,
You splendid prophets of immemorial springs
To come. Unfurl your tatters of woodsmoke
And glory and open the sky for the snows
Of our sleeping.

HYMN TO ORTHODOXY
Mother of Wars

I'm having a Druid up for tea
On Tuesday week, at half past three.
A Haida friend may also come
And bring along the Tabard nun
(Who took such a shine to that Dalai monk
She smuggled him home in her dowry trunk).
A Voodoo priest may also be there,
And just to keep it doctrinally fair
I'm asking the Pope and a Mandan chief
In case we run short of comic relief.
I'll save a spot for the Ayatollah
On Tammy's lap (on the sexional sofa).
Of Visigoths I'll invite a trio,
The Missouri Synod for brass (con brio),
A deputation from Salt Lake City,
And the Inquisition to preach on pity.
From Guyana I'll summon a chap named Jones
With a basket of toxins, skulls and bones—
And we'll gild a fleece for Ritzy Rajneesh
Who tethers God on a silken leash
And shows us how to massage our souls
While cruising in one of his fourteen Rolls.

At five, when done with our tea and crumpet,
I'll tootle a hymn on my terminal trumpet,
Condemn the allure of my Uncle Belial
And groupy indulgence in evil collegial—
And bang a big drum as we bury the Bestial,
Then sign us all up for the Neo-Celestial!

L'ENVOI

If *your* sect has said to Truth, "Come hither!"
May the Righteous squirm, the Omniscient wither;
For truth has many a seed unknown
That won't take root if wrongly sown.

NOW AND AGO

A Love Song of Sorts, at Seventy-five.
(Think of it)

Now was a time I remember well,
Or think I do at any rate.
Now was mostly for fun, I thought,
Unless I'd been drinking or up too late.

But suddenly *Now* has disappeared.
There's no time left between next and then:
I just lean over to tie my shoe
And it's time for love or art again.

I think it has something to do with quarks
And what goes on in outer space.
Everything's flying away from each.
There's trouble in keeping the stars in place.

Nothing holds still for a leisure look—
Streams run faster to fill up the sea
(And that's the place for sure, I'd guess,
Where *Now* will be waiting for you and me.)

I'd almost rather, for a while at least,
Be a fly in amber, a feather in space,
Could I only know where *Now* has gone
And why I'm waving my arms in place:
Wondering here, as the heart slows down

(But the pace picks up and less is more)
Why I'm suddenly missing so much,
And looking forward to that New Shore
Where *Now* will be with us forevermore.

REQUIEM WITH FIVE GRACES

This year I shall not know October's joyous
Outcry in the trees, nor, in spring,
The streamside's golden greening.
I shall have gone to earth and air by fire,
To that quiet place where leaves lie waiting, sleeping.

And I shall go down with Gratitude long honed
By sentience keen to Beauty's rich
And wayward heart: with gleaming
Reason as my guide: in Light, not dark:
With Hope in the long, long vigil I'll be keeping.

LOOKING INTO WOODS

LOOKING INTO WOODS

For R. F. and J. B.

Retrospectively

As down the rutted timber road I tread,
Beyond our last year's withering waste of slash,
I stop to peer into the uncut hardwood stand.
The pruning winds of March are hushed for now.
The sky's own light is welcome still
On naked twig and whip, branch and bole,
All wintered clean and waiting leaf.

Now's my fleeting chance to see the woods
For what they are: the clear anatomy of trees
Still free of greening billows hindering sight
And sky until October flings its palette
On the hills, the leaves to earth, and rime
Foretells the shroud of snow.

So now I go with grace to summer's peace
All reassured that Form still reigns with Reason
In the stern morphology of trees, trees
That I'll not see again till cold blows
Woodwinds in the air next fall, reminding
Me to pass this way once more for looking
Back in time, and into woods, with love.

DANCE OF THE FIDDLERS

The dance floor shines, tilted slightly
To the east, gentling the Atlantic
Back home, tide after tide, an eon's task.

From a dunebank's miniscule dressing room
Pop up two pillared eyes, bewaring
Gulls. The dancer steps out,

Sidles a step or two, testing sand:
Scuttles sidewise to tide line,
Legs a blur. His quickstep etches tracks,

Darts, stops. The war claw waves
Like Priam's shield, while the busy one
Flicks tidbits of sand flea and sea marsh

To the little maw, like the fist
Of a naughty Capuchin at the popcorn bowl.
What whimmery his dancing speaks!

When the night is bright, scores of them sweep the moon,
Crescendos of soundless shadows together
Bewitching the mud with deft

Ballet, grazing, racing the wavelets.
How is it they command my love,
Wordlessly, so much, each a

Bowlegged spring-toy of wonder, so serious
In their puttering on the tilting rims
Of our mother realm, their sea:

Indeed how wondrous altogether these skittering
Comics, trailing their tiny witness of love
Across the sand flats of infinity.

DOWNSTREAM

(For the Young Among Us)

Brooksong fails downstream, sensing marsh.
Bereft of bar and shallow, riffles glide
To sheen alone in the level long field's deeping.

Here, under the greencurved meadow's brink, a trout
Slinks, stalks a May-fly dimple. His gulp swirls,
Curls, rides to level, slides to oblivion,
Seabound.

He who is conned by the brook's upstream babblesong
(What it trills of tinkle and buttercups)
Better remember the dark and the deep,
Downstream.

IN PRAISE OF SYCAMORES

Zacheus he
Did climb a tree
Our Lord to see.

—The New England Primer

Zacheus was smart. Legend says
It was a sycamore he climbed, tallest
Of our deciduous trees, so big it is
Known that a man once lived inside one.
It's the most beautiful too, some say, its bark
Of dappled moonlight glowing even in
The sun, its limbs dark and akimbo
Against the sky: strong and beautiful
Enough to hold God, I'd say. Mostly
It's a solitary tree here in New England,
But along Missouri River bottoms the land's
Too rich not to grove. Peel a log
Of green sycamore and you'll see flesh
Like the rippled muscle of a skinned-out
Buck here in our November barnyard.
                        I hope some day
An honest somebody from Washington
Will ask me how I'd vote for a National Tree.
Thumbs up for Sycamore, I'd tell him.
I'd even offer to come to town and mount
A lobby. There's a lot of the American ideal
In this tall tree, straight and handsome,
Ready to grove or go it alone if need be.
The limbs retell the grief and fortitude
They've seen in our years together,
Their harsh and angled symmetry speaking
Hope and patience to those who've lost their way.
                        So I'd claim that

Zacheus knew what he was seeking
When he climbed aloft to look for God
In the great sycamore whose bark
Of crumpled starlight and mighty arms still
Speak Jehovah's word that we and God
And the earth are one, now and always.

INSHORE

As the racing water slid back to the wave line
It sucked the sand from around his bare feet,
Making him lose his balance for a moment,
As if the world were shifting under him.
The incoming windrow of fog seemed eerily
Incandescent, backlit by the sun's rising
Beyond the far white heave of the surf.
The receding sand tilted him again.

By now the fog had almost hidden
The off-shore breakers, billowing softly toward him
And the land, bringing a new chill.
He wondered if this were like the dying
He'd thought about so many times.

The sliding water whispered about his ankles
Again, tugging, as the cooling mist
Moved all around him, crowding over the dunes
And, beyond, inshore, over the silver-shingled village
It knew so well.

MINISTRY

I feel her presence in the half-lit quiet
Of the hospital night. She moves to my side,
Her feet shod with whispers, this white nun
Of mercy, substantial wraith who bears
The tiny plastic chalice of oblivion I crave.

Mother in white stockings, hair drawn and pinned:
But for her hands, there is all stiff coolness
Of starch in the whiteness of her, so wise
And deft of touch in the manifold skills
Of her impartial ministry.

I lie back and whisper thanks, but she is gone.
The drawn shades await sleep and
The joyless interminable graying of the day.

ANVIL AND STAR

For Salisbury
1741–1991

Three stars awake.
Two rivers sing.
Beyond a lake
New anvils ring.

White steeples soar.
A school is born,
An inn, a store,
A barn for corn,

Three homes, a street:
A rising sun
Then smiles to greet
A town begun.

In such simple ways
Those deeds of man
Enriched the days
Which hope began
In one small town
When rivers sang
Beyond a lake
Where anvils rang.

ANOTHER TIME

There, near me as I drowse
In a haze of autumn noon,
A slow glide of swans drift in a mist
Of silence on the unbroken river,
Wide here between fields.

And beyond them, on either side,
Hills, low as in sleep,
And far voices calling over the meadow
From loves left somewhere long ago,
Grieving still in a shadowy wood
Beyond the lulling water.

How strange are the dim low voices
That trouble the hills
And the tremulous waters of earth,
And why must they so throng my air and ear
Now in this dwindling light
Of my own life lost in a nameless wood,
Or under the darkling waters
Of another time?

SCALE

In the lamplight I contemplate
The shinbone of a mouse,
The ribcage.

I think jaguars, condors, anacondas,
Periwinkles, ladybugs. Then
I think frogspawn in the May pond's
Cool green. I think beauty.
Then I think scale: blindness:
The curved infinities of time, space,
Space-time: my blindness.

And I know then what God will say one day.
He'll say, "I want you to listen
To what the shinbone speaks of galaxies,
Helices, quanta, light beyond the stars.
Listen hard for the lost harmonies of Gaia
In your earth. Close your eyes and don't worry
About time, for time is only My way of making sure
Everything doesn't happen at once.
Now back to your lamplight and the magic
In the bone."

I'll think of God much harder then.
Bless Him for all this.

THE DOUBLE DUSK

The going up or coming down
Of sun on lake and field and town
Has never puzzled me a mite—
When I could tell the day from night.

I knew that dawn preceded day
When eastward coral banners lay,
And dusk was prelude to the close
When in the west there flamed the rose.

The light and dark are now in doubt.
The day and night are turnabout.
I cannot hope to know when smog
Is night or noon, or simply fog.

I know not much of good report
When comes the hour we must unsort
By vanished voice of owl or lark
The double dusk of dawn and dark.

SLOWER THAN WAKING

Slower than waking after love, more gently
than a new rose unfolds:

slower than the hemlock root's dark seeking
for water under dry stars, the rasp
of crickets:

slower than answers when eyes
look down in grief,
and the sun fails into autumn's western wood:

slower than all these I turn
from dreams to find
you gone.

NO MESSAGE

He admitted to himself, as he had not
to Emilia, that there could be no turning back,
no letter, no word, no message left
with friends. The future, he had learned,
was still a very large place, easy for losing,
traceless, yet bulging with wonderment and chance.

He got into the battered pickup,
slammed the door twice to make it latch,
stepped on the starter. It shuddered into reluctant
clatter. He laid his rumpled cap
on the seat beside him and eased the
stick-shift into low. He and the truck
moved resolutely out of the farm driveway,
up onto the blacktop, eastbound.

CHAOS AND I
or
The Limits of Perception

In the flailing wind
Snow veers, tumbles, leaps,
Flings a feathery veil of silver chaff
Against our house and barn, the huddled hills.

Now within my skull another storm is born
And churns, a reeling spate of dreams at risk
And mad hallucinations: kaleidoscopes
Of fractured light and soundless screams.

Never had I to discern the rift
Between old order and the turbulence in mind
Or thing. How clear it was! Some things
Changed, as flowers, bloomed and drooped,
And some like mountains stood eternal, sure.

Now a book I bought has done me in.
Atoms dance, I find. A thing's a process.
Bellying clouds and whorls in streams
Are brothers to the market trends and to
Fluctuations in our stock of doves or worms.

Weather, wind, the very stars a-wing,
The shapes of flame, all tumult, flow and stasis
Since the tides began, all, all,
All rocks and bells and maids and men
Are partners in the cosmic jig of microbits
In ceaseless motion toward the dark horizons
Of a universe whose newest name is flight.
As if this were not enough to stretch my
Aging arms around, I see erased the
Comfort line between things that used to
Bend to laws we knew, and those like

Waterfalls or summer storms whose gross
And wondrous antics never mattered then.

Now the new Equation Boys all claim to
Know the number keys to this bizarre behavior,
And thus can break the Universal Order Code
Of all we thought disordered in the world.
How dull, I say, to unitize the old familiar
Scene wherein we once enjoyed the chance to
Differentiate that which was rebel to established
Terms of Newton's will from that which
Still behaved in modes it always had: predictably.

So I must read another book, non-linear of course,
And bring myself in line to sup
At Lorenz's heady board whence butterflies
Send fractal signals off to storms
Three thousand skies away—and, the storms obey!

REFLECTIONS

On an invitation to the Catskills

My dear Ruth,
  How nice of you to think of me, stuck here in this little
country town at vacation time in June with so little to do.
But I'm afraid I must decline.
  June is such a lovely month here, and I really shouldn't
leave. How about October—late October? Let me know if
it's convenient. Or another year perhaps?

Thanks and all best
Randy

June, month of black flies and drooping peonies,
Is inserted between May and July,
Too late for real flowers, too early for dry heat.
It is devoted largely to ritual launchings
Of one kind or another, all with a
Dreary sameness: older school children,
Distracted with thoughts of imminent license,
Suffer the antique directives of dignified
Tycoons who have made it, entering and
Departing gymnasia on the measured wings
Of the Trumpet Voluntary. Eligible nubilistes
Rock and ecstasize to the most notable band
Daddy can afford, in tent or club.
Brides culminate, throwing bouquets
And kisses, expensively, memorably.
Little boys are deposited at quasi-wilderness
Cabins for the first rites of flannelhood
Before boarding school.
                    And out there, everywhere,
The tense business-like elation of tourists
Launching themselves, video-ready,
At Yellowstone, Disneyland, Mt. Rushmore,
Cape Cod, and other cultural zones where
The wildlife, the forest, or the slot-machines
Need attention.
                    The annual diaspora
Of healing and restoration is under way.

[174]

THE COMMITTEE OF LESSER BIRDS

Two sparrows primp and fluffle
in a puddle after rain. They are Thelma and Roland.

Madame Cowbird, having a moment ago left two eggs
in a neighbor's nest, demurely waits her turn as

Ronald Starling waddles aimlessly about
the Facility, displaying his yellow spots.

In a willow overhead, Chairman Raoul Crow
impatiently times the avian ablutions, cruckling
that, as usual, the Meeting of the Committee
of Lesser Birds will be late, late, late.

At last, they wing away to the Board Room
deep in a tree of thorns in the Dark Wood
where The Agenda waits.

Lesser Birds?

Ha!

REVEL

The wind,
Drunk with moonlight,
Stumbles among the trees.
The prim stars look the other way,
Sighing.

FIRST LIGHT: MONTAUK BEACH

Looking east from the slanted sand
My eyes go dim in first light.

The beach rises gently, swelling westward
To lift the first ancient breasts
Of the land, the sea-gift of dunes.

Inshore, far from the creaking of kittywakes,
There whispers the soft wishing of spent surf
Along the roll and rise of the slow hills,
The sighing of sea-shroud in the morning's
Cool and sibilant caress.

And out there, over the restless sway and surge
Of moving prairie, pacing the shorebound march
Of spume (or is it wheat?),
Beyond the nothing of horizon
Or under the sounding swell
And tremulous veil of water and sky,
I think I hear the beckon of that tranquil dark
That I shall know
One day.

SOLUTION

The sun disrobes, prepares to set.
Street girls descend to cast the net.
A priest intones the sundown mass.
The barkeep breathes upon the glass.

And I, who've seen this play before,
Shall watch it only one time more,
Then dim the lamp and pull the shade
To hide the drawing of the blade.

TWELVE: THIRTY-ONE: NINETY-NINE

A gray man on this Last Day
Shuffles into sunset.
He drags a sack heavy with
Withered hours,
   Dreamshards,
     Bangles,
      Icons,
        The ash of flags,
          The dry husks of two millennia.

Beyond the sunset
He will set his burden down beside a dead child
Where there is no history, no returning,
No light to the east.

And that will be that.

NORTHERING

In memory of the Eskimo Curlew, now extinct.

Beyond our April beach, along an inshore bar,
Tracing the silent chart of sun and star,
Three skeins of curlews grace my searching eye
With curves of flickering sickles in the sky.

These northering ones are led by tundra's lodestone
Call to follow where the prismed air's own
Clarity of frost and light is best
For brooding, best for sure tranquillity of nest.

And as they pass, they etch on air dark thoughts
For me, which speak familiar tales of avian fate.
I who fondly mark their sure and ancient flight
Hope them a lover's charm against that pathless night.

Printed from
Baskerville and Bulmer types
at The Stinehour Press.
Designed by Jerry Kelly.